The Graphic Novel

JACK
AND THE
BEANSTALK

CAST OF CHARACTERS

THE MOTHER

JACK

The Graphic Novel

JACK AND THE BEANSTALK

RETOLD BY BLAKE A.HOENA

ILLUSTRATED BY RICARDO TERCIO

www.raintreepublishers.co.uk
Visit our website to find out
more information about
Raintree books.

To order:
☎ Phone 0845 6044371
🖨 Fax +44 (0) 1865 312263
✉ Email myorders@raintreepublishers.co.uk

Customers from outside the UK please telephone +44 1865 312262

Raintree is an imprint of Capstone Global Library Limited, a company incorporated in
England and Wales having its registered office at 7 Pilgrim Street, London EC4V 6LB
Registered company number: 6695882

Editor: Laura Knowles
Art Director: Heather Kindseth
Graphic Designer: Kay Fraser
Librarian Reviewer: Katharine Kan
Reading Consultant: Elizabeth Stedem
Printed and bound in China by CTPS

ISBN 978 1 406 24319 2 (paperback)
16 15 14 13 12
10 9 8 7 6 5 4 3 2 1

British Library Cataloguing in Publication Data
Hoena, B. A.
Jack and the beanstalk. -- (Graphic spin)
741.5-dc23
A full catalogue record for this book is available from the British Library.

THE GIANT'S WIFE

THE GIANT

Once upon a time, a boy named Jack lived with his poor, widowed mother in England.

A man-eating giant had killed Jack's father some years ago.

The giant stole everything the family owned, except for their cow, Milky White.

Jack and his mother lived off the milk that Milky White produced.

Until one morning . . .

Not a drop!

Later that day . . .

Where are you off to this morning, young man?

I'm going to market to sell the family cow.

I could save you the trip. I'll swap you that old cow for these . . .

Oh, all right!
Come along then.

You'd better eat up quickly before my husband comes home.
Yes, ma'am.

21

The next morning, Jack decided to visit the castle one last time.

He wanted to get back the last of his father's belongings.

He snuck inside and hid in a large teapot just before the giant arrived.

FEE FIE FOH FUM!

I smell the blood of an Englishman!

On the giant's command, his golden harp sang a lovely tune.

Sing!

Soon, the giant began to fall asleep . . .

LA-LA-LA-LA-LAAAAA

The giant that killed Jack's father had now come to his own end. By selling the hen's golden eggs, Jack and his mother became very, very rich.

And they lived happily ever after.

ABOUT THE AUTHOR

When Blake A. Hoena was growing up, he wrote stories about robots conquering the Moon and trolls lumbering around in the woods behind his parent's house – and the fact that the trolls were hunting for little boys had nothing to do with Blake's pesky brothers. He then went on to study for a Master of Fine Arts degree in Creative Writing. Since graduating, Blake has written more than thirty books for children, including retellings of "The Legend of Sleepy Hollow" and the Perseus and Medusa myth. Most recently, he's been working on a series of graphic novels about two space alien brothers, Eek and Ack, who are determined to conquer our big blue home.

ABOUT THE ILLUSTRATOR

Ricardo Tércio is a freelance illustrator from Lisbon, Portugal. He co-founded a production company and has made animation and videos for some of the top Portuguese musicians. Tércio also illustrated for large companies such as Hasbro. In 2007, he illustrated his first comic, *Spider-Man Fairy Tales #1*, for Marvel.

GLOSSARY

beanstalk stem of a bean plant

belongings items that a person owns

command order someone to do something

fearful scary, or something that causes fear

harp large, triangular musical instrument that is played by plucking its strings

ma'am polite title for a woman

market place where people buy, trade, and sell food or goods

produce make

rightfully if an object is rightfully someone's, it belongs to that person

widowed if someone is widowed, his or her husband or wife has died

THE HISTORY OF JACK AND THE BEANSTALK

Fairy tales were always told and retold orally before being written down. Each time different storytellers retold the fairy tale, they often added a new detail or changed events slightly. They did this to make the story more exciting, more interesting, or more to their liking. For these reasons, there are several versions of fairy tales such as JACK AND THE BEANSTALK.

"The History of Mother Twaddle, and the Marvellous Atchievements of Her Son Jack", by B. A. T., appeared in the early 1800s. In this version of the story, a servant girl, not the giant's wife, lets Jack into the castle. Also, Jack kills the giant by beheading him.

Another version printed in the early 1800s was by Benjamin Tabart. In his retelling of JACK AND THE BEANSTALK, a fairy tells Jack that the giant had killed and stolen from his father. Tabart added this detail to give Jack a reason for stealing from the giant.

In 1890, Joseph Jacobs published a different retelling of the fairy tale. He based it on a version of the story he remembered from his childhood. In his retelling, Jack steals from the giant because he is a trickster and a misbehaving boy. There is no mention of Jack's father at all.

Today, Jacobs' **JACK AND THE BEANSTALK** is thought to be the closest to the original version, though no one knows for sure. The version you just read is most similar to Tabart's version of the tale, but even in it, the author has changed some details. Jack's mother, not a fairy, tells Jack that the giant has their family treasure.

DISCUSSION QUESTIONS

1. Jack trades the family cow, Milky White, for a handful of "magic" beans. If you were Jack, would you have done the same thing? Why or why not?

2. Do you think it was right for Jack to steal from the giant? Explain your answer.

3. Fairy tales are often told over and over again. Have you heard the Jack and the Beanstalk fairy tale before? How is this version of the story different from other versions you've heard, seen, or read?

WRITING PROMPTS

1. Write a story about what would have happened to Jack and his mother if he had not traded Milky White for the magic beans. What would Jack have received for Milky White instead? How would he and his mother have survived?

2. Imagine that you lived up in the clouds like the Giant and his wife. Write about your life there. Describe the scenery, plants, and animals. Are there any special activities you would do because you lived in the clouds?

3. The story ends by saying that Jack and his mother lived happily ever after. But did they really? Write a story about what happens to Jack and his mother after the giant dies. Does Jack fight other monsters or marry a princess? Does he go back up into the clouds or have other adventures?

OTHER BOOKS IN THE SERIES

Beauty and the Beast	978 1 406 24317 8
Red Riding Hood	978 1 406 24772 5
Sleeping Beauty	978 1 406 24771 8

MORE FAIRY TALES TO ENJOY

The book may be over, but the adventure is just beginning. There are many other exciting and fantastical tales for you to discover:

Grimm's Fairy Tales (Usborne Illustrated), Ruth Brocklehurst (Usborne, 2010)

Hans Christian Andersen's Fairy Tales (Usborne Illustrated), (Usborne, 2011)